Peru

Anita Croy

Hildegardo Córdova Aguilar and David J. Robinson, Consultants

NATIONAL GEOGRAPHIC
WASHINGTON, D.C.

Contents

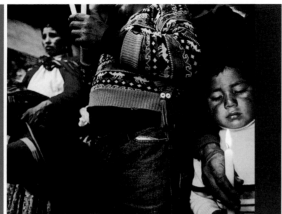

Contents **3**

Peru is the third-largest country in South America, after Brazil and Argentina. It is also one of the most popular: Over a million foreign visitors arrive each year. They mainly come to see the Andes Mountains and the ruins of Peru's ancient cultures. But Peru has far more to offer, from thick rain forest to cities with fashionable restaurants and shopping boutiques.

Peru's geography is made up of great contrasts. Peruvians live in a variety of landscapes—coast, highlands, and rain forest—but the majority live near the Pacific coast in the west. In Peru's modern cities, many people enjoy a way of life similar to that in other developed countries.

The variety of landscapes makes Peru one of the most biodiverse countries of the world. It contains all of the major types of biome, from tropical forests to frozen glaciers. The rain forest that covers about 60 percent of Peru is home to more than 1,200 native plant species, 450 birds, 102 mammals, 69 reptiles, 58 amphibians, and 256 fish. To preserve such biodiversity, Peru has created more than 12,355 square miles (32,000 square kilometers) of natural reserves, of which the largest are Tambopata and Pacaya-Samiria.

The highest mountain chain in the tropical world, the Andes has supported several historical cultures, of whom the Inca were the most important. Around their capital at Cusco, the Inca farmed on terraces cut into the hillsides. Like their predecessors, they were skilled farmers and domesticated many crops, such as potato, corn, quinoa, kiwicha, oca, olluco, squash, pepper, and cotton. Peru's later history was shaped by Spanish domination, which played an important part in forming modern

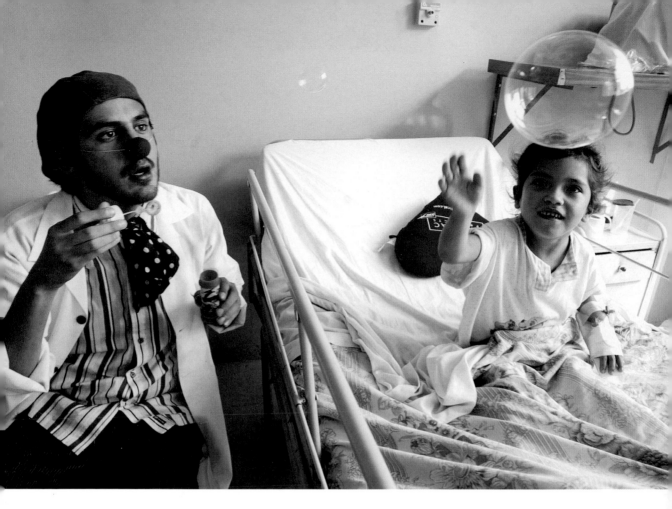

Peruvian culture. Today's daily life in Peru reflects Spanish and Inca traditions, as well as the influence of globalization.

I hope you enjoy this book. And I hope that some day we get to welcome you to Peru to enjoy the beauty of our landscapes and the friendship of our people.

Dr. Hildegardo Córdova Aguilar
Executive Director
Center for Research in Applied Geography
Pontiphical Catholic University of Perú

▲ **A Peruvian doctor entertains a young patient. Better health care for everyone is one of the main challenges for Peru.**

From Desert to Jungle

HIGH IN THE ANDES of Peru, the mountains are so tall and forbidding that the ancient Inca people used to worship them as gods. Less than 100 miles (160 km) to the west, sea fogs cling to the Pacific coast. Especially in winter, they cover the capital, Lima, and the coastal plain with mist so thick that people cannot see the sun clearly for months at a time. Along much of the coastal plain, deserts stretch right to the edge of the ocean. It is hard to tell where the beach ends and the desert begins. On the eastern side of the Andes lies a vast jungle, part of the Amazon rain forest. The forest is home to birds and animals that do not live anywhere else on Earth. Native Indians live among the trees and have little contact with modern ways of living.

◀ The Andes, the second-highest mountain range in the world, divide Peru into western and eastern sections that are so different they could be separate countries.

WHAT'S THE WEATHER LIKE?

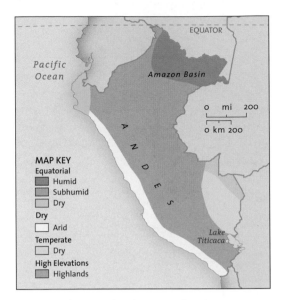

Peru's climate depends on which part of the country you are in. In the high mountains, it snows all year round. Although it is often dry and sunny, it can get very cold. In the jungle, it is hot and humid all the time, but heavy rains fall between December and March. The most unusual weather occurs on the Pacific coast. Between May and November much of the coast is covered in a thick mist, known as *garúa*. The map opposite shows the physical features of Peru. Labels on this map and on similar maps throughout this book identify places pictured in each chapter.

Fast Facts

> **OFFICIAL NAME:** Republic of Peru
> **FORM OF GOVERNMENT:** constitutional republic
> **CAPITAL:** Lima
> **POPULATION:** 28,302,603
> **OFFICIAL LANGUAGES:** Spanish, Quechua
> **MONETARY UNIT:** Nuevo Sol
> **AREA:** 496,224 square miles (1,285,216 square kilometers)
> **BORDERING NATIONS:** Bolivia, Brazil, Chile, Colombia, and Ecuador
> **HIGHEST POINT:** Mount Huascarán, 22,205 feet (6,768 meters)
> **LOWEST POINT:** Pacific Ocean, 0 feet (0 meters)
> **MAJOR MOUNTAIN RANGE:** Andes
> **MAJOR RIVERS:** Amazon, Ucayali, Madre de Dios

Average Temperature & Rainfall

Average High/Low Temperatures; Yearly Rainfall

Lima (Pacific Coast)
77–82° F (25–28° C) / 53–59° F (12–15° C); 2 in (5 cm)

Cusco (Central Highlands)
68° F (20° C) / 52–55° F (11–13° C); 32 in (82 cm)

Arequipa (Southern Highlands)
73° F (23° C) / 42° F (5° C); 4 in (9 cm)

Iquitos (Jungle)
100° F (37.7° C) / 59° F (15° C); 103 in (262 cm)

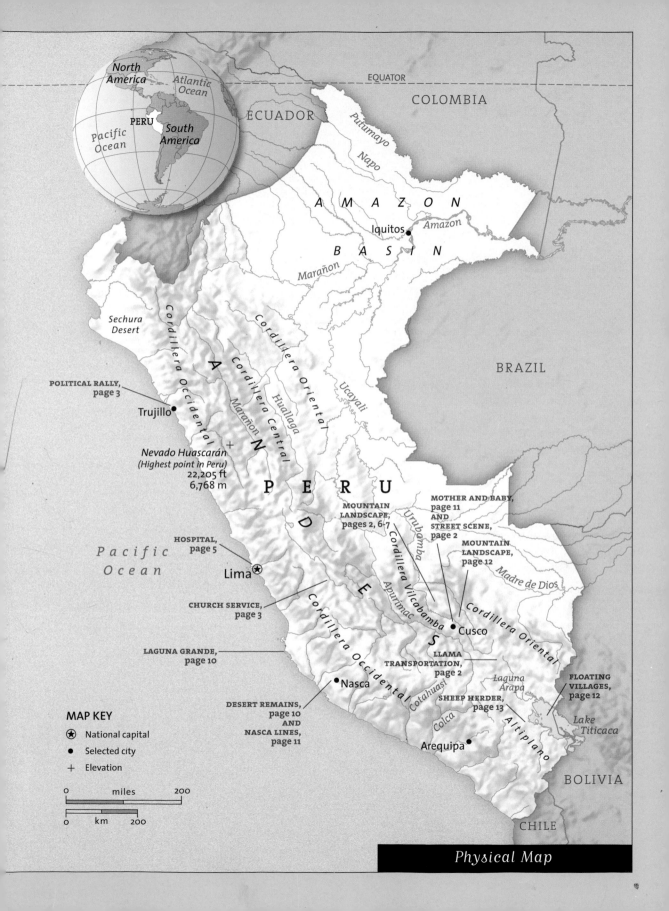

North America

Atlantic Ocean

PERU

Pacific Ocean

South America

EQUATOR

COLOMBIA

ECUADOR

Putumayo

Napo

A M A Z O N

Iquitos● *Amazon*

B A S I N

Marañon

BRAZIL

Sechura Desert

Cordillera Occidental

Cordillera Central

Cordillera Oriental

Huallaga

Marañon

Ucayali

A

POLITICAL RALLY, page 3

Trujillo●

N

Nevado Huascarán
(Highest point in Peru)
22,205 ft
6,768 m

+

P E R U

D

MOUNTAIN
LANDSCAPE,
pages 2, 6-7

MOTHER AND BABY,
page 11
AND
STREET SCENE,
page 2

MOUNTAIN
LANDSCAPE,
page 12

Urubamba

Madre de Dios

Pacific Ocean

HOSPITAL,
page 5

Lima⊛

E

CHURCH SERVICE,
page 3

Cordillera Occidental

Cordillera Vilcabamba

Apurimac

Cordillera Oriental

●Cusco

LAGUNA GRANDE,
page 10

S

LLAMA
TRANSPORTATION,
page 2

Laguna Arapa

FLOATING
VILLAGES,
page 12

●Nasca

SHEEP HERDER,
page 13

Cotahuasi

Altiplano

Lake Titicaca

MAP KEY

⊛ National capital

● Selected city

+ Elevation

DESERT REMAINS,
page 10
AND
NASCA LINES,
page 11

Colca

Arequipa●

0   miles   200

0   km   200

BOLIVIA

CHILE

Physical Map

The Coast

Peru's west coast bordering the Pacific Ocean is a narrow strip of desert about 1,555 miles (2,500 km) long. Thousands of years ago, ancient peoples settled in the valleys of the rivers that flow from the Andes to the ocean.

▲ Desert dunes tower over the tiny fishing port of Laguna Grande on the Pacific Ocean.

▼ The deserts of the southern coast are so dry that ancient remains like this Nasca burial site have been preserved for centuries.

The small areas of fertile land along the rivers supported cultures such as the Chimú and Nasca. The desert makes up only 10 percent of Peru's area, but it is home to more than half of all Peruvians. In the 1980s and 1990s, many people moved here to cities such as Lima, the capital, and Trujillo to find work. The coastal strip is mainly dry and dusty, and gets cool and damp in the winter. Faults in the Earth's crust run along the coast. When the huge plates on either side of the faults slip, they cause earthquakes, which strike Peru several times in each decade.

The south coast is drier than the north. The dryness has helped preserve the mysterious Nasca Lines, giant sand markings that cover an area of nearly 200 square miles (500 sq km). The seventy shapes include animals and plants, as well as long straight lines, triangles, and other geometric shapes. Each figure is made from one continuous line. The drawings are so big that it is impossible to make out the shapes from the ground. Many were first seen when an airplane flew over the desert in 1920. Archaeologists still wonder who drew the lines and why—and how the drawings were so accurately done.

The Mountains

The Andes run from north to south. The mountains are so high that on a clear day they can be seen by people 50 miles (80 km) away on the beaches of the Pacific. The Inca city of Machu Picchu lay hidden in the mountains for over three hundred years. Other ancient sites may yet be discovered. The highest peak, Mount Huascarán, is 22,205 feet (6,768 m) high. It is still worshiped by

THE DESERT WITH NO SUNSHINE

Most people think of the desert with a blazing sun beating down on lots of sand. In Peru, the desert can be very different. Between May and November, the coastal desert is covered in thick sea fog that does not move for weeks at a time. This fog, called garuá, is created when cold seawater meets the dry desert air. The thick cloud hangs over the coast, making everything seem gray. Drops of water from the mist cling to the leaves of desert plants, providing them with a valuable source of moisture.

◄ **A pair of archaeologists in red jackets look tiny as they measure the dimensions of one of the Nasca figures—a giant spider!**

some Indian peoples.

As well as high mountains, the Andes also contain two of the world's deepest canyons. In southern Peru, close to the city of Arequipa, is the Cañón del Colca (Colca Canyon). It is twice as deep as the Grand Canyon in Arizona. North of Arequipa, the recently explored Cañón de Cotahuasi (Cotahuasi Canyon) is even deeper.

▲ At twilight, Andean peaks have a magical glow. It is easy to see how people can consider them sacred.

THE FLOATING ISLANDS OF LAKE TITICACA

Lake Titicaca is so big that it looks almost like a sea. It is impossible to see from one side to the other. The lake holds a special position in myth, as the birthplace of the first Inca.

Some seventy islands in the lake are home to the Uru people, whose ancestors have lived there for over 10,000 years. The islands are special because they are artificial. The Uru make them from floating beds of reeds. Over time, the reeds at the bottom rot in the water, so the islanders often add new reeds to the top. Today, tourists can stay with families on the islands, and this is the main way the islanders earn their living.

▲ An Uru man steers his boat toward his village, which is built on an island of matted totora reeds.

Even today, it is difficult to cross the Andes from east to west because there are few paved roads or railroads over the mountains. Flying is the easiest way to get from one side of the country to the other, but it is too expensive for most Peruvians.

Mountain Life

People who visit the mountains often suffer from altitude sickness. The air is so thin that they find it hard to breathe enough oxygen. They get tired and breathless. Over centuries, the highlanders who live on the slopes east of the Andes have gotten used to the conditions. They chew coca leaves to combat the effects of altitude. The Indians raise alpacas and llamas for meat and wool, and grow potatoes and barley for food. They farm just as their Inca ancestors did centuries ago. They cut flat terraces into the slopes like giant steps where they can grow crops.

In southern Peru, Quechua- and Aymara-speaking Indians live on the Altiplano, a high, flat plateau

▲ A shepherdess tends her sheep in the Altiplano, the highlands east of the Andes. Only hardy animals thrive on the scrubby grassland, known as puna.

between ranges of the Andes. The region has been home to people for thousands of years. The Inca believed that humans were first created at Lake Titicaca, the world's highest navigable lake, which lies 12,497 feet (3,809 m) above sea level.

Selva, High and Low

When people think of Peru, they usually think of mountains. But more

▲ Thunderclouds darken the sky above the Amazon River. The jungle gets about fifty times more rain than the coast.

than half of Peru—60 percent—is covered by selva, dense, wet forests. So-called high selva grows in the mountains, while low selva grows in valleys and basins. The low selva is part of the world's largest rain forest, the Amazon, which also covers nearly half of Brazil. The rain forests contain more varieties of animal and plant life than any other habitat. Some species have not yet

A LONG WAY TO LIMA

Traveling in Peru from north to south has been easy since ancient times. Today, the Pan-American Highway runs along Peru's Pacific coast as part of its journey from Alaska and Canada in the north to Argentina in the south. But the great barrier of the Andes still makes crossing Peru from east to west difficult for people who cannot afford to fly.

During the rubber boom of the nineteenth century, people rushed to Amazonian cities like Iquitos hoping to make their fortunes. If they had to visit Lima, the capital, about 600 miles (965 km) away, the mountains made a direct journey impossible. The only way to get from Iquitos to Lima was to travel by boat down the Amazon to the Atlantic Ocean, then north along the South American coast. After crossing Panama by land, travelers took another ship south to Lima. To travel 600 miles actually took a journey of some 7,000 miles (11,260 km).

Today, there are three highways across the Andes. They link the cities of the coast to river ports in the Amazon basin.

been recorded or named. Scientists think that there may still be Indian groups deep in the selva who have never met an outsider.

Deep in the rain forest in northeast Peru, the city of Iquitos stands on the Amazon, the world's longest river. It is only connected to the capital, Lima, by air. The city was built in the 19th century during a rubber boom. Today, it is the fifth-largest city in Peru and a center for oil exploration. Companies are building roads and pipelines to get the oil out.

Biologists call the forests of the lower slopes of the Andes cloud forests because they lie at altitudes where damp mist often cloaks the slopes, giving many plants their moisture.

▲ On the old waterfront of Iquitos, wooden huts stand on stilts at the river's edge or even float on rafts. The inhabitants get around in motorized canoes.

A Diverse Natural World

FOR THE ANCIENT MOCHE, llamas were so precious that people sacrificed them to please the gods. For centuries, the llama has carried heavy loads and provided meat, milk, and thick wool for people in Peru's highlands. Today they still carry goods in areas with few roads. The rich natural world has supported Peruvians for centuries. Peru has a wider variety of animals and plants than most other countries because it is home to more than three-quarters of the world's different biomes, or habitats. Many species are unique, particularly in the Amazon rain forest. Unlike people in other countries, Peruvians have not made a great impact on natural life. In the high mountains and the deep jungle, humans have barely disturbed the natural world.

◀ Llamas and alpacas—their close relatives—are driven across the dusty plains of northern Peru on their way to market.

DIVERSE ECOSYSTEMS

The map opposite shows Peru's main vegetation zones—or what grows where. Vegetation zones form ecosystems. Peru has a wide range of ecosystems because of its great variation in elevation, or height above sea level. They range from cold Pacific waters in the south to warm tropical seas in the north, from coastal deserts to the steep Andes and highland plateaus, and from dry tropical forests to rain and cloud forests. Such a range of habitats means that Peru is one of the most biologically diverse countries in the world: It is home to 472 species of mammal—about a third are different sorts of bat. Almost one-fifth of all bird species in the world fly through Peru. And some species may not yet have been discovered!

▶ Sea otters were hunted for their skins until the 1970s, but hunting them is now illegal.

Species at Risk

Because so much of Peru is hard for humans to get to, animal and plant life have largely been able to flourish. This might change before too long, however. Environmentalists are worried about the impact drilling for oil and gas will have on the rain-forest ecosystem. Along the coast, pollution is a possible problem because of the overcrowded cities and concentration of industry. The following species are among those at risk:

> Anderson's mouse opossum
> Short-tailed chinchilla
> Spiny rat
> Yellow-tailed woolly monkey
> Andean cat
> Blue whale
> Incan little mastiff bat
> Giant armadillo
> Giant otter
> Marine otter
> Mountain tapir
> Pacarana (rodent)
> Peruvian fish-eating rat
> Ucayali spiny mouse

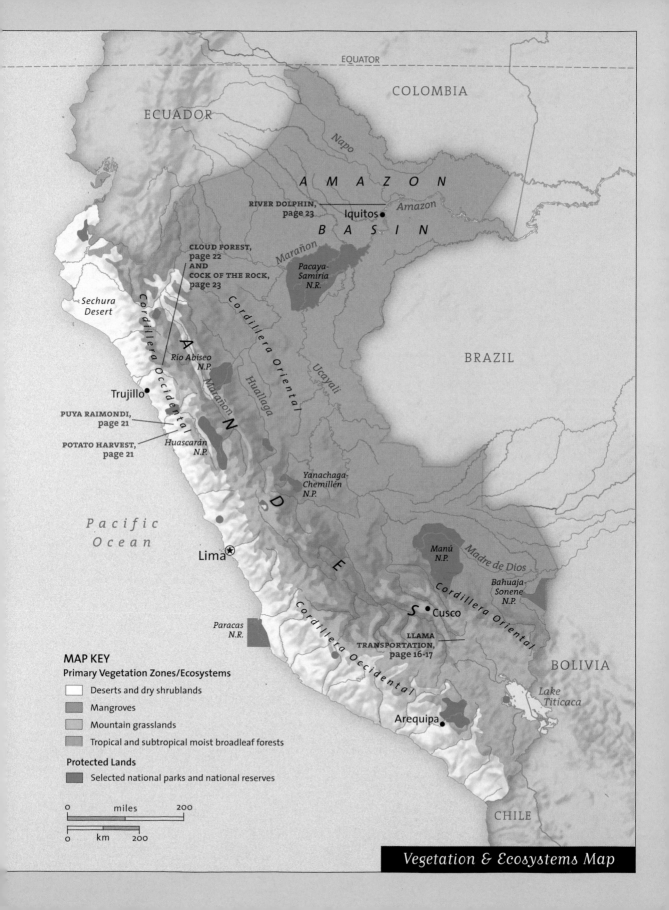

EQUATOR

COLOMBIA

ECUADOR

Napo

A M A Z O N

RIVER DOLPHIN,
page 23

Iquitos • *Amazon*

B A S I N

Marañón

CLOUD FOREST,
page 22
AND
COCK OF THE ROCK,
page 23

Pacaya-
Samiria
N.R.

*Sechura
Desert*

Cordillera Occidental

Cordillera Oriental

A

*Río Abiseo
N.P.*

Ucayali

BRAZIL

Trujillo •

Marañón

Huallaga

N

PUYA RAIMONDI,
page 21

POTATO HARVEST,
page 21

*Huascarán
N.P.*

D

*Yanachaga-
Chemillén
N.P.*

*Pacific
Ocean*

E

Lima ⍟

*Manú
N.P.*

Madre de Dios

Cordillera Oriental

*Bahuaja-
Sonene
N.P.*

S • Cusco

*Paracas
N.R.*

Cordillera Occidental

LLAMA
TRANSPORTATION,
page 16-17

BOLIVIA

*Lake
Titicaca*

Arequipa •

CHILE

MAP KEY

Primary Vegetation Zones/Ecosystems

- Deserts and dry shrublands
- Mangroves
- Mountain grasslands
- Tropical and subtropical moist broadleaf forests

Protected Lands

- Selected national parks and national reserves

0   miles   200

0   km   200

Vegetation & Ecosystems Map

Desert and Ocean

It almost never rains on Peru's long coast, and plants are rare in the coastal deserts. The main sources of moisture are the sea fogs that form in some regions, where they support shrubs on raised hillocks called *lomas*. In the north of Peru, little grows on the giant sand dunes. Beyond the desert, however, grows *bosque seco* (dry forest), which is home to a mesquite shrub called algaroba. As the coast becomes less dry in the far north, there are mangrove swamps.

The seas off Peru are rich in life. The Peru Current that runs north along the coast draws cold water from the deep ocean to the surface. This water is rich in nutrients that support small life-forms, which in turn are food for huge numbers of fish such as anchovies and sardines. Almost a fifth of the world's food fish are caught around the Peru Current. The fish attract large numbers of seabirds and marine animals. In the late nineteenth century, there were so many birds that guano (bird droppings, used as a fertilizer) made Peru very rich.

The Sierra

In the mountains, plants that have adapted to high altitudes grow up to an elevation of about 16,000 feet (4,875 m). Above such heights, snow and ice lie throughout the year, and only lichens and mosses can survive. The puna grasses that grow above about 13,000 feet (3,960 m) provide grazing for llamas and alpacas and their wild relatives, the vicuña and guanaco. The most famous plant of the puna is the puya raimondi, which takes up to one hundred years to bloom. Before it dies it puts on a spectacular show. It grows a giant spike up to 27 feet (10 m) tall, with 20,000 blooms.

On the slopes of the highlands, Indian communities grow the vegetables that form the main part of their diet: potatoes, quinoa (a grain crop), and corn.

The Tropical Forests

Nearly two-thirds of Peru is covered by tropical rain forest or cloud forest. One patch of selva measuring

▲ A puya raimondi blooms only once in a century.

▼ Farmers in the highlands store great piles of potatoes, one of their staple foods.

CLOUD FOREST

Peruvians call the forest that grows on the lower slopes of the Andes, between about 3,500 and 9,000 feet (1,200 m–3,000 m), the "ceja de selva" or "eyebrow of the jungle." That is because the forest clings to the steep slopes along the valley bottoms.

The way the cloud forest plants get their moisture is very different from plants in the lowland forests. There is less rain; instead, as warm jungle air rises over the mountains and cools, mist forms over the cloud forest. Plants such as ferns, mosses, and orchids have adapted to absorb moisture not through their roots—some have virtually no roots at all—but through their leaves. The cloud forest has more species of orchid than anywhere else on Earth. It is also home to one of the world's rarest plants, the giant begonia.

The cloud forest is very special because it contains so many unique species of plants as well as many different species of animals. Endangered species such as the *pudú* or pygmy deer and the spectacled bear, which is the same size as the North American black bear, live in the forest. The bright body and crest of the cock-of-the-rock, Peru's national bird, can be spotted in the trees. It is one of the world's most plant- and animal-rich environments. Scientists have not identified all the species yet, and there is a race against time to catalog them all before some of the species are destroyed.

▼ Mist rises from the cloud forests of the Andes at sunset. Some plants in the forest are epiphytes: They do not have roots but absorb moisture from the damp air through their leaves.

just 250 acres (100 ha) is home to more than 6,000 kinds of plants! Such variety makes the Peruvian jungle important for our understanding of life on Earth.

The tropical rain forest is swampy, with slow-moving rivers. In the north of Peru is the Amazon rain forest. On the Amazon River, which is over a mile (1.6 km) across in places, visitors pass through deep jungle. They will probably see monkeys, alligator-like caimans, hundreds of types of birds, lots of butterflies (Peru has 20 percent of the world's butterfly species), and also the world's largest rodent, the capybara. The capybara looks like a large guinea pig and grows to the size of a hog, weighing as much as one hundred pounds (45 kg). It lives in the water, and its meat is very popular with Amazonian peoples.

▲ The cock-of-the-rock, Peru's national bird, lives in the cloud forests, where it nests on rocky cliffs.

THE HOT-PINK DOLPHIN

About twenty years ago, biologists working in the Amazon could not believe their eyes. On a home movie filmed near Iquitos was a creature they thought was extinct: the pink dolphin.

The pink dolphin is found only in Amazonian rivers around Iquitos. It may get its color from blood capillaries near its skin. Unlike other dolphins, it has a hump instead of a fin and a long bottle-nosed snout rather than a short one. It swims alone more often than the more common gray river dolphin.

Because the pink dolphin is so rare, local Indian peoples think it is sacred. There are lots of myths and stories attached to the animal that the locals call *bufeo*.

▲ The pink dolphin's hump and long snout help it search for shellfish and small fish.

Empires
and
Ruins

WHEN SPANISH TROOPS entered the Inca capital of Cusco in 1532, they could not believe their eyes. The city glittered with gold. Its buildings were magnificent and its roads better made than any in Europe. It was ten times bigger than the most important city in Spain at the time, Madrid.

The Inca were just one of the early civilizations that built empires in Peru's difficult terrain. None had a written language, and archaeologists are still learning about them from the ruins and objects they left. Many of the Quechua-speaking peasants of Andean Peru are Inca descendants. Other Peruvians are of European descent. Their ancestors were the Spanish conquerors who were another great influence on modern Peru.

◀ An Andean woman in traditional dress walks along a street in Cusco. Alongside her is a wall built by her Inca ancestors over five hundred years ago.

EARLY CULTURES

▲ Using terraces to grow crops on steep hillsides was a key step in the development of Peru's early cultures. They produced food to support settled communities.

Peru is a very old country. The earliest inhabitants arrived there about 15,000 years ago. The earliest developed societies emerged between 3000 and 1800 B.C. They are known as pre-ceramic peoples, because they did not know how to make pots. The evidence of their existence made archaeologists change their ideas. They had always assumed that knowing how to make pottery was an essential part of early societies.

The first societies lived on the coast. The people were nomads, who moved around rather than living on settled sites. They survived by hunting and fishing in the fish-rich Pacific Ocean. They later moved into the river valleys that led down from the highlands. They learned how to domesticate crops such as cotton and how to terrace and irrigate their fields. The development of farming allowed the people to build fixed settlements. The Inca later built complex canal systems to irrigate their crops.

At the same time, new societies emerged along the coast. Their remains are not as well preserved as those of the highlands, so it is harder to know how they lived.

Time line

This chart shows the various cultures that dominated Peruvian history after 1000 B.C. The most famous civilization, the Inca, was also the briefest, lasting barely a century.

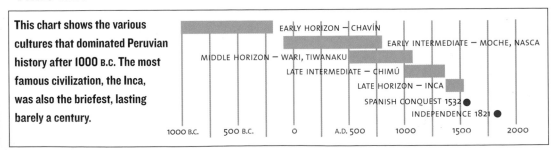

EARLY HORIZON — CHAVÍN
EARLY INTERMEDIATE — MOCHE, NASCA
MIDDLE HORIZON — WARI, TIWANAKU
LATE INTERMEDIATE — CHIMÚ
LATE HORIZON — INCA
SPANISH CONQUEST 1532 ●
INDEPENDENCE 1821 ●

1000 B.C. | 500 B.C. | 0 | A.D. 500 | 1000 | 1500 | 2000

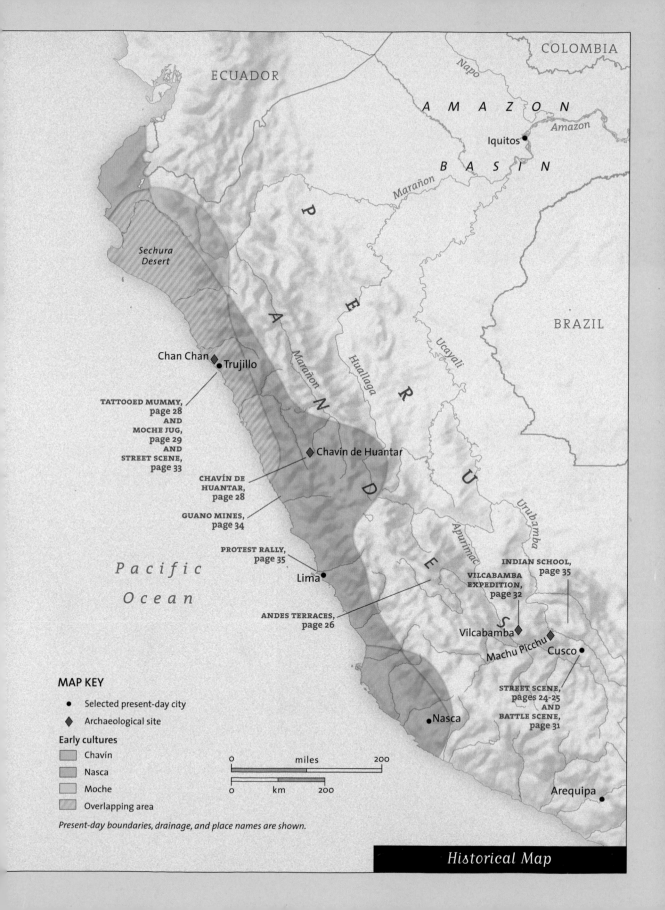

COLOMBIA

ECUADOR

Napo

A M A Z O N

Amazon

Iquitos

B A S I N

Marañon

P

E

Sechura
Desert

R

BRAZIL

A

Marañon

Huallaga

Ucayali

Chan Chan
Trujillo

N

TATTOOED MUMMY,
page 28
AND
MOCHE JUG,
page 29
AND
STREET SCENE,
page 33

Chavin de Huantar

D

U

CHAVÍN DE
HUANTAR,
page 28

GUANO MINES,
page 34

Apurímac

Urubamba

PROTEST RALLY,
page 35

Pacific

E

INDIAN SCHOOL,
page 35

VILCABAMBA
EXPEDITION,
page 32

Lima

Ocean

ANDES TERRACES,
page 26

S

Vilcabamba

Machu Picchu

Cusco

STREET SCENE,
pages 24-25
AND
BATTLE SCENE,
page 31

Nasca

MAP KEY

- ●   Selected present-day city
- ◆   Archaeological site

Early cultures

	Chavín
	Nasca
	Moche
	Overlapping area

Present-day boundaries, drainage, and place names are shown.

Arequipa

0   miles   200

0   km   200

Historical Map

First Civilizations

One of the first great civilizations to emerge in Peru was the Chavín, who built an empire between about 1000 and 200 B.C. that stretched through the north and central highlands and along the coast. The Chavín worshiped nature spirits and buried their dead with feathers and a shiny black stone named obsidian. Such objects came from the rain forests to the east, showing that the Chavín traded beyond the Andes.

Of the civilizations that followed, two of the most important were the Moche and the Nasca (100 B.C.–A.D. 800). The Nasca were based in the south, where they created the mysterious lines in the desert. To the north, the Moche were an urban civilization who had much in common with the later Inca.

▲ A young boy visits Chavín de Huantar, a temple built in about 850 B.C. It is one of the oldest ruins in Peru.

MYSTERY OF THE TATTOOED MUMMY

In 2006, archaeologists discovered a Moche tomb on the Pacific coast that contained the mummy of a woman. She was so well preserved that tattoos on her arms are still visible. The woman was buried with valuable goods, so she must have been important. The discovery suggested that the Moche might have had female leaders, not just men as had been previously thought.

▲ Tattoos of snakes and spiders on the mummy's arm

Early Empires

In the highlands around Lake Titicaca, the Tiwanaku emerged after about A.D. 500 to conquer a large empire. Like the Wari, who built their own empire about a century later, the Tiwanaku grew quinoa and built stone cities. Both empires set examples for the Inca. They used warfare to conquer their neighbors and built stone-paved tracks between their cities. The Wari kept records using knots in colored strings, called quipu. The Inca did the same.

Rivals

On the coast of Peru, the Chimú ruled an empire between 1000 and 1470 from the royal city of Chan Chan, which was home to as many as 100,000 people. The Chimú grew rich from trade and tribute. Tribute was a way of taxing conquered people, who had to give crops or treasure to the Chimú. Meanwhile, a small group named the Inca began to take power around the highland city of Cusco.

Almost unknown before 1430, within about fifty years the Inca had taken control of the territory of many of their neighbors, including the Chimú. They absorbed many Chimú practices into their own society.

A Mighty Empire

The Inca called their empire Tawantinsuyo, Quechua for "The Four United Regions." At its peak, it stretched from Colombia to Chile and east into Bolivia and Argentina. The Inca forced their defeated enemies to pay taxes, known as *mita*, through labor and produce. The Inca collected vast amounts of food from those they conquered.

▼ This detail of a ceramic bottle shows how skilled Moche potters were at capturing human expressions.

THE ICE MAIDEN

A remarkable discovery in 1995 shed new light on Inca beliefs. While climbing high on Nevado Ampato, a volcano in the Andes, archaeologist Johan Reinhard and a companion found a wrapped bundle in the ice. When they turned it over, they were stunned to find themselves looking at the face of a young girl. The freezing temperatures at the top of the mountain had preserved the body—Reinhard nicknamed her Juanita—for over 500 years.

Juanita had been killed as a sacrifice to the Inca gods. Reinhard has found other frozen children on other mountains. He believes that some parents even offered their own children to be sacrificed. The victims were dressed in beautiful clothes and led in a procession to the top of the mountain, where they were killed outright or drugged so that they fell asleep and died.

◄ Juanita's mummy gave archaeologists new clues about how the Inca dressed and even what they ate.

The Inca built stone roads, which are still used today, to connect parts of the empire with Cusco, home of the emperor. Cusco's walls still stand, despite several earthquakes. Their huge stones fit together so well that it is impossible to slip a piece of paper between them.

The Inca built their empire without either the wheel or a written language. They kept records with quipu—but were still able to rule a vast area.

Spanish Conquest

After only about one hundred years, the Inca empire fell apart as fast as it had developed. In 1532 Spaniards, led by Francisco Pizarro, landed on the coast. The sight of the Inca emperor Atahualpa sitting on a golden throne, covered in jewelry, dazzled Pizarro. The Spaniards seized the emperor and demanded gold and silver to set him free. The Inca paid the ransom, but Pizarro still killed Atahualpa. Atahualpa's brother, Manco Inca, fled into the mountains of Vilcabamba.

Why Did the Inca Fall?

Pizarro had overthrown an empire with fewer than 200 men and sixty horses. Historians have often wondered how the Spaniards defeated the Inca so easily. One

▼ Spanish soldiers turn on Inca guarding Atahualpa. After the conquest, the Spaniards treated the Indian peoples badly, forcing them to work in mines and on sugar plantations.

▲ Archaeologists camp at Vilcabamba on an expedition to investigate the end of the Inca empire. The Inca lived on in the mountains until their final defeat by the Spaniards in 1572.

explanation may lie in an Inca myth that said that a god would one day appear from the Pacific with pale skin and a beard—just like Pizarro. The Inca may have believed that the god had come. But the most likely explanation is disease. The Inca had no immunity against common European diseases such as smallpox or influenza. Contact with the newcomers meant death for millions of people.

From Vilcabamba, Manco Inca resisted the Spanish. But in 1572 the invaders gained control of the whole empire after they killed his successor, Tupa Amaru.

Colonial Rule

Spain ruled Peru for almost three hundred years. Spanish immigrants became Peru's elite. As Spaniards and local people married, their children became known as mestizos (of mixed blood). Lima became capital of the Viceroyalty of Peru, which covered much of South America. The city grew rich because all goods sent to or from Spain had to pass through it.

The Spanish forced local people to work, often in hot, filthy gold and silver mines. The city of Potosí, now in Bolivia, became the richest town in the world. Its silver mines kept Spain rich.

Independence!

By 1780 the Viceroyalty of Peru was in decline. A sign of growing unrest

TUPA AMARU

The first Tupa Amaru was the last Inca temperor. From Vilcabamba, he led resistance to the Spanish before his execution in 1572.

Two centuries later, in 1780, an Indian leader fighting the Spanish rulers claimed to be a descendant of the Inca and took the name Tupa Amaru II. He led local people in a brief uprising against Spain, but he was captured and executed in 1781.

The uprising encouraged Peru's independence movement. For Peruvians today, the name Tupa Amaru is still closely linked with resistance to oppression.

◄ A Spanish colonial cathedral dominates a city square in Trujillo. The European settlers built churches like the ones they had at home and forced the native Peruvians to convert to Christianity.

MONEY FROM BIRD DROPPINGS

The millions of seabirds that teem above Peru's coastal waters leave tons of droppings (guano) along the coast and its islands. The ancient Moche used the droppings as fertilizer but, in the 19th century, guano briefly became the basis of Peru's whole economy. It was in great demand in Europe, to help grow crops to feed the rising population. By 1849, nearly all of Peru's income came from guano. When the invention of artificial fertilizers in the 1870s ended the demand for guano, Peru fell into debt.

▲ Guano was loaded onto ships at docks like these and shipped to Europe.

came with the Tupa Amaru II rebellion. The revolutions in America (1776) and France (1789) encouraged Peruvians to start hoping for independence.

Two soldiers eventually drove Spanish troops from Peru. Neither of them was Peruvian. Simón Bolívar, a Venezuelan, and the Argentine, José de San Martín, attacked Lima from the sea. Peru declared its independence on July 28, 1821.

The New Country

Between 1826 and 1895, Peru had thirty-five presidents, including Simón Bolívar. Many had fought for independence. They were called *caudillos*, or strong men. Other military men have governed Peru since. Today, many people still prefer to have a strong president.

Independence did not change life for most Peruvians. The elite still ran the country, and the Indians had little power. The economy depended on resources such as guano or rubber. There were booms when everyone wanted Peru's exports, but they were followed by busts when the market collapsed, making Peru poor again.

After 1879, when it was defeated in the War of the

Pacific, Peru lost valuable land to the victor, Chile. The British helped the Peruvians pay their debts, but in return took control of resources such as the railroads.

Toward Reform

In the 20th century, Peru was split between a rich elite, who mainly lived in Lima, and the poor majority. Politicians found it difficult to make lasting changes to society. In 1924 Victor Raúl Haya de la Torre formed the APRA party to stand up for Peru's workers. The government used illegal ways to stop the party from getting power, including killing its leaders. It was only in 1985 that APRA had a president elected.

A violent attempt to change Peru came in the late 1980s and 1990s, when terrorists from an organization called Shining Path attacked government targets. The government defeated them and also tackled inflation, or rising prices, and corruption. The changes will help get the economy into better shape and improve life for all Peruvians.

▲ One of the greatest challenges for political reformers in Peru is to educate Indian children, whose families often prefer them to work rather than go to school.

▼ A man carries his baby at a rally to protest terrorist attacks by the Shining Path group in the 1990s.

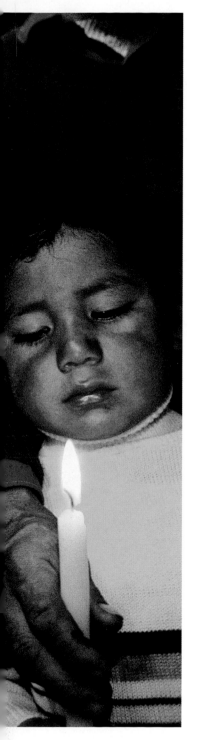

Different Pasts, Shared Future

WALK DOWN ANY BUSY street in Lima and you will see all sorts of faces. Indians, Spaniards and other Europeans, descendants of African slaves, and later arrivals from countries like China and Japan have, over time, married and created modern Peruvians. In the words of a popular song, *"El que no tiene de Inga, tiene de Mandinga"*—a Peruvian who does not have an Inca ancestor will have Mandinga or African roots.

Whatever their background, Peruvians agree on the importance of family and religion. Generations of a family often live and work together and look after each other in hard times. Many Peruvians are very religious. Most follow the Catholic faith introduced by the Spanish.

◄ **A Quecha family attends Mass in a highland church. Many Peruvians combine Christian faith with older beliefs, as in the celebration of the Day of the Dead.**

RURAL AND URBAN POPULATION

Until nearly the end of the twentieth century, Peru was a rural country. Most people lived outside the cities, which, with the exception of the capital Lima, were small. Since the 1970s, the population has grown quickly. It is just over 28 million today.

Nowadays most people live in cities, mainly on the coast. Many families moved there to find work. Lima is the most densely populated city, with eight million citizens. In contrast, the jungle that covers about 60 percent of Peru is home to only 6 percent of the country's population.

▶ A shoeshine boy makes his way home from the city. Children from poor families often find ways to make extra money for their parents.

Common Peruvian Phrases

The official languages of Peru are Spanish and Quechua, but many people speak other indigenous languages, such as Aymara. Here are some common Spanish phrases you might hear in Peru:

Buenos días (bweh-nos DEE-ahs) Good morning
Buenas noches (bweh-nas NOCH-ez) Good evening
Hola (OH-lah) Hello
Adiós (ah-dee-OS) Goodbye
Qué tal? (KAY tal) How's it going? How are you?
Por favor (pohr fah-VOHR) Please
Gracias (GRAH-see-us) Thank you
De nada (di NAH-dah) No problem, you're welcome

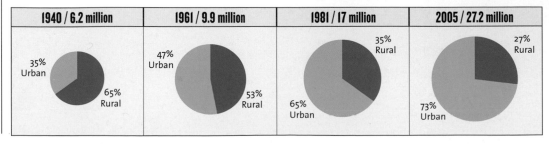

1940 / 6.2 million	1961 / 9.9 million	1981 / 17 million	2005 / 27.2 million
35% Urban / 65% Rural	47% Urban / 53% Rural	35% Rural / 65% Urban	27% Rural / 73% Urban

COLOMBIA

ECUADOR

Tumbes

Talara
Sullana
Paita • Piura
Catacaos

Jaén
Chachapoyas
Chiclayo
Cajamarca

Moyobamba
Tarapoto

Iquitos

BRAZIL

MOCHE BOTTLES,
page 42

Trujillo

Chimbote
Huaraz
Huánuco
Cerro de Pasco
Barranca
Huacho
Huaral
Callao
Lima

Tingo María

Pucallpa

Pacific
Ocean

Tarma
Huancayo

CHURCH SERVICE,
pages 36-37

FAMILY IN
CANOE,
page 44

MACHU PICCHU,
page 44

SCHOOL CHILDREN,
page 41
AND
SOCCER MATCH,
page 45
AND
SURFERS,
page 45

Huancavelica
Imperial
Chincha Alta
Pisco
Ica

Ayacucho

Cusco
Abancay

Puerto
Maldonado

INTI RAYMI,
page 43

SHOESHINE BOY,
page 38

Juliaca
Puno

Arequipa

BOLIVIA

Moquegua

Ilo
Tacna

CHILE

| miles | | 200 |
| 0 | km | 200 |

People per
square mile

Over 2500

626–2499

61–625

12–60

Under 12

People per
square kilometer

Over 1000

250–999

25–249

5–24

Under 5

MAP KEY
Population of urban area

▪ Over 5 million

▲ 500,000 to 1 million

● 100,000 to 500,000

• Under 100,000

Population Map

► Children often help their families work. This family is heading into the rain forest to help harvest mahogany, one of the most valuable types of timber.

NATIONAL HOLIDAYS

Holidays in Peru mark both religious and nonreligious celebrations, such as the achievement of independence.

JANUARY 1	New Year's Day
FEBRUARY/MARCH	Carnival
MARCH/APRIL	Holy Week (Semana Santa)
	Easter
MAY 1	Labor Day
JULY 28	Independence Day
AUGUST 30	Santa Rosa de Lima's Day
NOVEMBER 1	All Saints' Day
NOVEMBER 2	Day of the Dead
DECEMBER 8	Feast of the Immaculate Conception
DECEMBER 25	Christmas

School Is Cool

For urban middle-class Peruvians, life is a lot like life in the United States. Children go to school, and their parents go to work. On weekends, they shop in malls and eat out in restaurants. Life is very different in the mountains, where many families find it hard to earn money. Their kids need to work rather than study. The law says that children must go to school from age six to fourteen, but that does not always happen.

In the cities, lessons are taught in Spanish. Children of Indian families who have moved from the mountains to find work speak Quechua or Aymara. They have to learn Spanish before they can understand the lessons. Many of them drop out of school by junior high to earn money to help their families. Children in richer families in Lima attend private schools, which can be very competitive.

Students who graduate from high school can choose between private and public universities. Peru had a university even before the United States: San Marcos University opened in Lima in 1551.

▲ Girls chat outside their school at the end of the day. More than 90 percent of Peruvians can read or write, although the average is lower among rural communities.

Catholics and Converts

The Spanish made Peruvians convert to the Catholic faith. Today, Catholicism is Peru's official religion and shapes daily life for millions of people. The Protestant branch of Christianity is also becoming more popular. Families go to church on Sundays and celebrate religious holidays during the year. In the mountains, Indian communities mix ancient beliefs with Catholicism to create a unique religion.

▲ Corn was the crop that sustained Peru's earliest settled cultures.

A HUNDRED COLORS OF CORN

The Spanish were amazed to discover that the Inca made ears of corn out of solid silver. For the Inca and other pre-Hispanic civilizations, corn was a sacred food. It still is today. It makes *chicha*, a drink like beer, which is popular at festivals. Before taking a sip, drinkers pour a little *chicha* on the ground in honor of Pachamama, the goddess of fertility.

Everyone has seen yellow or white corn, but in Peru corn also comes in shades of blue and purple. Purple corn is used in a dessert called *mazamorra morada*. *Choclo* is a toasted cob of corn served with cheese and chili sauce.

The potato originated and was domesticated in the Andes. Early peoples buried potatoes with their dead as food for the afterlife. Today, more than 200 varieties of potato grow in Peru, including purple and yellow ones. There is even a practice in the highest Andean villages of setting potatoes in the sun to dry and then leaving them out overnight to freeze. The "freeze-dried" potatoes can then be stored for several years.

▼ Bottles made by the Moche for storing *chicha*, a sacred drink made from corn.

A Varied Menu

Peru has some of the most varied food in the world. What Peruvians eat depends on where they live. On the coast, where seafood is plentiful, one of the most popular dishes is ceviche: raw seafood mixed with lime juice, hot peppers, and onion. In the mountains, where potatoes and corn are staple foods, people cook a special meal called *pachamanca* that takes all day to prepare. A big hole is dug in the ground and lined with hot stones. Then different sorts of food like meat, beans, potatoes, sweet potatoes, and *humitas* (corn cakes) are put inside, and the hole is filled in. The food cooks slowly for many hours, but by the end of the day it is very tasty.

Fiesta!

Across Peru it seems as though there is always some kind of festival happening. The most famous fiesta is carnival, the period before Lent, with processions, music, and drinking and eating. Lent ends with one of the biggest festivals in Peru: Semana Santa, or Holy Week. It seems like all of Peru is on vacation as people visit their families and watch

▲ Colorful costumes, masks, and dancing are an important part of many fiestas.

◀ Peruvians re-enact Inti Raymi, a ceremony their Inca ancestors used to honor the sun.

MACHU PICCHU

▲ Machu Picchu stands on a high ridge above a bend of the Urubamba River.

Machu Picchu is the most spectacular of the many sites the mighty Inca left behind. Today it is the most popular tourist destination in South America and one of the most famous archaeological sites in the world. Thousands of people visit every day, but one hundred years ago the ruins were home to only a couple of Indian farmers. The American explorer Hiram Bingham discovered the "lost city" of Machu Picchu in 1911. He could not believe how well preserved it was, or how precisely its big, irregular stones fit together.

Machu Picchu stands on a mountaintop in the Urubamba Valley, but at a lower elevation than the imperial city of Cusco. The Inca used the city to escape Cusco's cold weather for around one hundred years. The Spanish never found Machu Picchu, and it remained undisturbed until Bingham stumbled across it. The precise purpose of the site is unknown. Perhaps it was a sacred place where the Inca could worship the sun. The layout of the city today is still almost exactly the same as it was in Incan times.

parades of Bible scenes. Another festival celebrates Peru's independence from Spain on July 28, 1821.

Music and Dance

One of the most important parts of any Peruvian party is music. Some highland instruments are found only in Peru, like the Andean harp, or *charango*, which resembles a ukelele. Other instruments are used more widely, such as panpipes and flutes. Andean people have at least 200 different dances. One of the most popular, the *huayno*, is danced all over the country.

On the coast, a new kind of music from the shantytowns of Lima is named after Peru's favorite corn beer. Chicha music mixes highland music with the music of Afro-Peruvians. These descendants of African slaves still use the same wooden box drums called *cajones* as their ancestors to beat out a rhythm.

Sports Crazy

Peru is soccer crazy. On Sunday, groups of boys and men get together to play "fútbol" in towns across Peru. The small team of Ciencano from Cusco hit the headlines in 2003, when they were the first Peruvian team to win the Copa Sudamericana, beating some of South America's best teams along the way.

Other popular sports include surfing. Kids in the coastal cities grow up right by the beach, and Peru has some of the world's best surfers. Mountain sports are very popular, too.

▲ A Peruvian defender tackles a forward from neighboring Bolivia.

▼ Peru is great for surfing—and not just for people. Chicama Beach has the longest waves in the world.

On the Comeback Trail

I N 2006, PERUVIANS RE-ELECTED the man who had become the country's youngest president ever in 1985. Few people had thought that Alan García Perez would make such a spectacular comeback. But in Peruvian politics, people have come to expect the unexpected.

When García was first president, terrorism, inflation, and corruption were crippling the country. Many farmers grew coca, which can be turned into the drug cocaine. But by the time García returned to power, the government had gotten rid of many corrupt officials and defeated Peru's terrorists. Farmers were destroying their coca plantations and planting other crops. As a result, Peru's economy was more stable than it had been for a long time.

◄ **The re-election of Alan García Perez in 2006 was a sign that Peruvians were hopeful the problems of his first term in office were a thing of the past.**

PILES OF PAPERWORK

Peru is divided into twenty-five regions and one province— the capital, Lima. The regions vary greatly in size. Loreto is the largest region, covering much of the Peruvian rain forest, but has only a small population. Lima has the country's largest population in a small area.

Peruvians often complain that nothing gets done by government without lots of paperwork. In some government offices, a worker does nothing but stamp the date on all the official papers that arrive each day. Now a big effort is being made to cut down on paperwork to help things run more smoothly.

▶ Shantytowns like Tupac Amaru may not enjoy the wealth of Peru's great urban centers, but their residents still have a strong sense of pride in their community.

Trading Partners

Peru traditionally exports more goods than it imports. The chief exports are fish and fish products from the Pacific, such as anchovies and sardines. Minerals such as gold, copper, and zinc are also important exports. In turn, Peru has to import consumer goods and industrial supplies.

Country	Percentage Peru Exports
United States	29.5%
China	9.9%
United Kingdom	9.0%
Chile	5.1%
Japan	4.4%
All others combined	42.1%

Country	Percentage Peru Imports
United States	30.3%
Spain	11.5%
Chile	7.2%
Brazil	5.4%
Colombia	5.2%
All others combined	40.4%

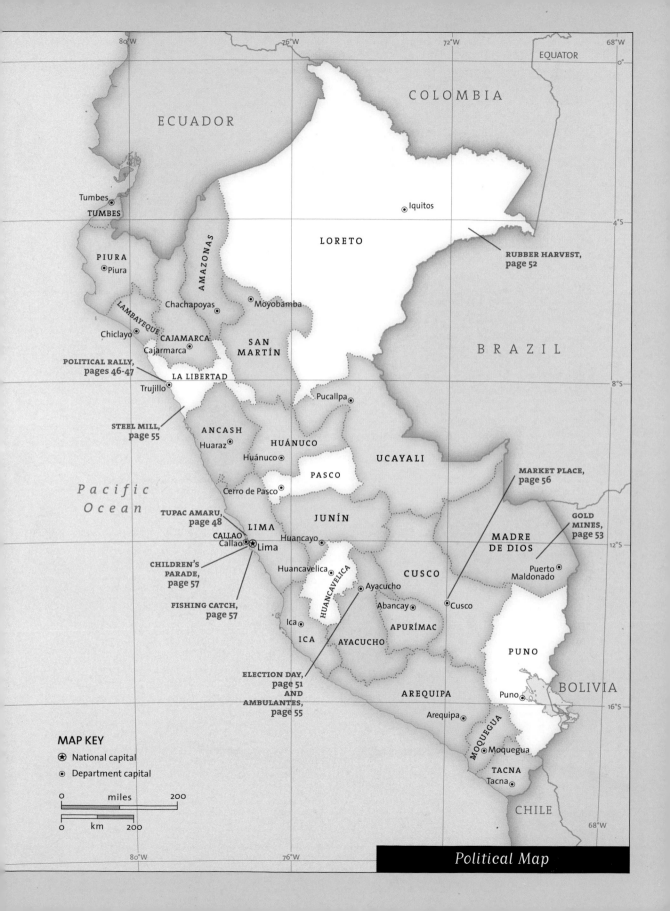

EQUATOR

80°W   76°W   72°W   68°W

COLOMBIA

ECUADOR

Tumbes ⊙
TUMBES

⊙ Iquitos   4°S

PIURA
⊙ Piura   LORETO
                                                    RUBBER HARVEST,
                                                    page 52
AMAZONAS

LAMBAYEQUE   Chachapoyas ⊙   ⊙ Moyobamba
Chiclayo ⊙   CAJAMARCA   BRAZIL
            Cajarmarca ⊙   SAN
POLITICAL RALLY,   MARTÍN   8°S
pages 46-47
            LA LIBERTAD
    Trujillo ⊙   ⊙ Pucallpa

STEEL MILL,
page 55   ANCASH
            Huaraz ⊙   HUÁNUCO
                    Huánuco ⊙   UCAYALI
Pacific   MARKET PLACE,
Ocean   PASCO   page 56
            Cerro de Pasco ⊙
                                            GOLD
TUPAC AMARU,   JUNÍN   MINES,
page 48   page 53
        LIMA   MADRE
CALLAO   DE DIOS
Callao ⊙ ⊛ Lima   Huancayo ⊙
CHILDREN'S   Puerto ⊙   12°S
PARADE,   Huancavelica ⊙   Maldonado
page 57   HUANCAVELICA CUSCO
FISHING CATCH,   Ayacucho ⊙
page 57   Abancay ⊙ ⊙ Cusco
        Ica ⊙   APURÍMAC
        ICA   AYACUCHO   PUNO
ELECTION DAY,
page 51   16°S
AND   AREQUIPA
AMBULANTES,   Puno ⊙   BOLIVIA
page 55
                    Arequipa ⊙
                                    MOQUEGUA
MAP KEY   Moquegua ⊙
⊛ National capital   TACNA
⊙ Department capital   Tacna ⊙

0   miles   200   CHILE

0   km   200   68°W

80°W   76°W

Political Map

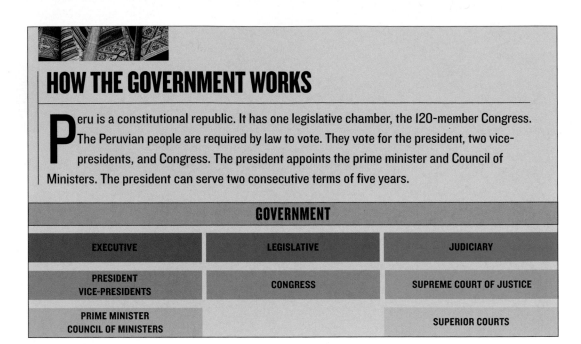

HOW THE GOVERNMENT WORKS

Peru is a constitutional republic. It has one legislative chamber, the 120-member Congress. The Peruvian people are required by law to vote. They vote for the president, two vice-presidents, and Congress. The president appoints the prime minister and Council of Ministers. The president can serve two consecutive terms of five years.

GOVERNMENT		
EXECUTIVE	LEGISLATIVE	JUDICIARY
PRESIDENT VICE-PRESIDENTS	CONGRESS	SUPREME COURT OF JUSTICE
PRIME MINISTER COUNCIL OF MINISTERS		SUPERIOR COURTS

Serving All the People?

Since Peru declared independence in 1821, many governments have found it difficult to work for all Peruvians. The split between the rich and the poor is very wide, and what benefits the rich may hurt the poor, while what might help the poor would only be paid for by taking money from the rich. Peru's first presidents were drawn from the small elite of landowners and military officers. These *caudillos* wanted to preserve their own wealth and that of their friends. The poor benefited little from their rule.

During the twentieth century, two presidents made particular efforts to help Peru's poor. Augusto B. Leguía, who ruled as a dictator between 1919 and 1930, brought in new laws to help workers and Indians. He did not have enough money to pay for his reforms, however, and was removed from power by a coup.

In 1968, the army general Juan Velasco Alvarado seized power. Everyone expected him to favor the elite, like other caudillos, but instead he passed laws to help the poor. He set up rural schools to give Indian children the chance to study. He gave workers more rights. Like Leguía, Velasco found that change was expensive. He did not have the money to see his reforms through.

At the end of the twentieth century, scandals surrounded the presidency of Alberto Fujimori, a Peruvian of Japanese descent. One of Fujimori's advisers was filmed trying to bribe a political opponent. Fujimori fled the country. Peruvians turned back to García Perez, who had served as president twenty years earlier.

THE COMEBACK KID

When Peruvians re-elected Alan García Perez as president in 2006, it was a remarkable turnaround. Back in 1985, at age thirty-six, García had become Peru's youngest president and the first member of the APRA party to hold the post. His plan to modernize the economy began well but then led to rapid price rises. Lots of Peruvians could barely afford food, with prices going up three times a day. The people turned against the president. When rumors began that he was corrupt, García fled the country.

In 2001, García returned to Peru. The country had changed. After a series of scandals, the government said that it had stamped out much corruption. Many Peruvians were happy to trust García again. The new president promised to build roads, schools, and health clinics in rural areas to help the poor.

◀ The voting forms in Peru's elections have pictures of the candidates so that even people who cannot read are still able to vote for their favorite.

▶ A worker uses a machete to slash the bark of a rubber tree to collect its sap. Harvesting rubber is hard work in the humid rain forests.

THE RUBBER BOOM

Peru has suffered from cycles of boom and bust as a result of its reliance on natural resources. One example came in the late nineteenth century. The invention of the tire for automobiles and bicycles led to a huge demand for rubber in Europe and the United States. Growers in Peru used low-paid native workers to harvest gum from the rain forest.

As prices rose, the isolated Amazon town of Iquitos became one of the richest places on the planet. Planters shipped luxuries there from Europe—even whole houses. But the boom was brief. The British used seeds from the Amazon to grow rubber trees in Asia. They flooded the market with cheap rubber, and Peru's boom was over.

Natural Wealth

Peru is one of the richest countries in the world in natural resources. Metals such as gold, silver, copper, zinc, lead, and iron are found across the country, and there are vast underground reserves of oil and natural gas. The cold waters off the coast are full of fish, which attract the seabirds whose guano brought Peru so much wealth in the nineteenth century. The rain forests of the Amazon are a rich source of valuable timber.

Despite all these natural advantages, for much of its history

Peru has been a poor nation. A series of booms in demand for its natural resources all ended when the international market no longer needed the product.

One crop that is worth a lot of money but that the government does not want to be grown is coca. Traditionally, Peruvians living in the highlands have grown coca leaves to chew because they help with hunger and altitude sickness. But the leaves are also used in the production of the illegal drug cocaine. As the price of the drug rose in the 1980s and 1990s, many Peruvian farmers were persuaded to grow the crop.

▲ This barren landscape was created by the effects of gold mining. Such large-scale projects can be disastrous for the local ecology. Conservationists are working to convince companies to operate in ways that damage the environment less.

The Informal Economy

Jobs in Peru can be hard to find. Many rural Peruvians who move to the cities have little education and find it difficult to get regular jobs. Some people have come

AGRICULTURE

The map shows where Peru's key plantation cash crops are grown. Sugar, cotton, rice, and fruit are among the main crops grown for export.

MAP KEY
Major Products
- Coca
- Cocoa
- Coffee
- Cotton
- Fish
- Rice
- Sugarcane

Pacific Ocean

Lima

Lake Titicaca

up with ways to find other work. In the cities, it is common to see *ambulantes*. These "street-sellers" are often children. They make money by selling gum or chocolate from trays they carry around. In Lima, unofficial taxis called *combis* compete with buses for passengers. Combis are all shapes and sizes— whatever the driver can get hold of.

This kind of job is part of the Informal Sector, the unofficial part of the economy where people pay no taxes. Experts think this may make up as much as 40 percent of Peru's economy. It is difficult to know for sure—no one keeps accurate records.

Another part of the Informal Sector is *trueque*. In the highlands, Indians often do not buy goods with money. Instead they trade them for other goods, for example swapping potatoes for cooking oil. This old system of bartering used to be common around the world.

Agriculture and Fishing

With Peru's different altitudes it is possible to grow almost anything. For centuries, a few landowners have owned nearly all the best farming land. They hire peasants to work for little money. Crops grown on the coastal strip such as asparagus, broccoli, sugarcane, rice, and cotton are mainly for export.

◀ A worker tends a furnace in a steel mill in Peru. About a fifth of the country's workforce is employed in industry.

▼ Ambulantes sell bread and candied apples on the streets. Recent reforms aim to make such workers legal—partly so that the government can collect taxes from them.

In the Andes, the Indian communities graze their livestock on the Altiplano. They grow crops for their own use and barter any extra with their neighbors.

Off the coast are some of the world's richest waters. Fish and fish products are two of Peru's biggest exports, but it is vital to look after stocks. Overfishing halved the catch by 1987. Since then, restrictions on fishing have given fish more chance to breed. The fishing industry has also suffered from the weather phenomenon known as El Niño, which makes the ocean too warm for fish.

Government & Economy   **55**

▲ A weekly market in the highlands offers a mixture of colorful produce.

A Promising Future

Peruvians are developing better ways to manage all their natural resources, from fish to gold, so that they can preserve supplies and reduce damage to the environment. They are also eager to break the boom-and-bust cycle by no longer relying so heavily on

AN UNWELCOME GIFT FOR CHRISTMAS

Fishers in Peru noticed that their catches sometimes fell around Christmas. They gave the phenomenon that caused the decline the name "El Niño," which means "Christ Child" in Spanish.

Scientists haved learned that every three to seven years the Pacific Ocean warms up off the Peruvian coast and fish cannot survive. El Niño also has effects on land. In 1997–1998, a strong El Niño led to heavy rain, flooding, and mud slides in northern Peru.

El Niño's effects are felt a long way from Peru. It affects the weather around the world.

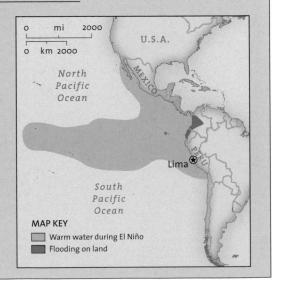

U.S.A.

MEXICO

North Pacific Ocean

PERU

Lima ⊛

South Pacific Ocean

0 mi 2000
0 km 2000

MAP KEY
▢ Warm water during El Niño
▢ Flooding on land

natural resources to earn foreign income. The huge gap between rich and poor is one of Peru's most serious problems. A more stable economy is the first step in helping the government plan ways to benefit the poorest citizens.

One promising development is tourism. In 2000, Peru had more than a million visitors for the first time. People from around the world are eager to see Peru's spectacular scenery and ancient ruins. Numbers are likely to keep rising—as long as visitors do not damage the very sites they come to see. Hikers to Machu Picchu, for example, have to take their trash away. There is no more room to bury it at campsites along the trail. It is a hard, four-day trek, but the path is always busy: The thrill of experiencing Peru's history is well worth the tired legs.

▲ A fisher carries his catch ashore. Fish and fish products are Peru's largest export.

▼ Indian children join a campaign to increase vaccination against polio; in some rural areas, use of Western medicines is rare.

Add a Little Extra to Your Country Report!

I f you are assigned to write a report about Peru, you'll want to include basic information about the country, of course. The Fast Facts chart on page 8 will give you a good start. The rest of the book will give you the details you need to create a full and up-to-date paper or PowerPoint presentation. But what can you do to make your report more fun than anyone else's? If you use your imagination and dig a bit deeper into some of the topics introduced in this book, you're sure to come up with information that will make your report unique!

>Flag

Perhaps you could explain the history of Peru's flag and the meanings of its colors and symbols. Go to **www.crwflags.com/fotw/flags** for more information.

>National Anthem

How about downloading Peru's national anthem, and playing it for your class? At **www.nationalanthems.info** you'll find what you need, including the words to the anthem in Spanish and English, plus sheet music for the anthem. Simply pick "P" and then "Peru" from the list on the left-hand side of the screen, and you're on your way.

>Time Difference

If you want to understand the time difference between Peru and where you are, this Web site can help: **www.worldtimeserver.com**. Just pick "Peru" from the list on the left. If you called Peru right now, would you wake whomever you are calling from their sleep?

>Currency

Another Web site will convert your money into nuevol sol, the currency used in Peru. You'll want to know how much money to bring if you're ever lucky enough to travel to Peru: **www.xe.com/ucc**.

>Weather

Why not check the current weather in Peru? It's easy—simply go to **www.weather.com** to find out if it's sunny or cloudy, warm or cold in Peru right this minute! Pick "World" from the headings at the top of the page. Then search for Peru. Click on any city you like. Be sure to click on the tabs below the weather report for Sunrise/Sunset information, Weather Watch, and Business Travel Outlook, too. Scroll down the page for the 36-hour Forecast and a satellite weather map. Compare your weather to the weather in the Peruvian city you chose. Is this a good season, weather-wise, for a person to travel to Peru?

>Miscellaneous

Still want more information? Simply go to National Geographic's One-Stop Research site at **http://www.nationalgeographic.com/onestop**. It will help you find maps, photos and art, articles and information, games and features that you can use to jazz up your report.

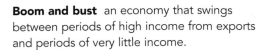

Glossary

Boom and bust an economy that swings between periods of high income from exports and periods of very little income.

Cash crop a crop that is grown to be sold.

Caudillo (Spanish for "strongman") a leader in a Latin American country who is often a former military officer.

Corruption using power to make money illegally for oneself or one's friends.

Coup the sudden removal of a government by a small group of people, often military officers.

Domesticate to breed or tame animals so that they live closely with humans.

Ecosystem a community of living things and the environment they interact with; an ecosystem includes plants, animals, soil, water, and air.

Endangered describes a species that is in danger of becoming extinct.

Extinct describes a species that has died out.

Fault a break in the Earth's crust along which movement occurs, causing earthquakes.

Habitat the environment where an animal or plant lives.

Irrigation using artificial canals or other ways to bring water to dry areas so that they are suitable for agriculture.

Mangrove a woody tree or shrub with roots that project above the mud, which grows on tropical coasts.

Mummy a dead body that has been well preserved.

Nature spirits spirits that are believed to dwell in natural features such as rocks, streams, or trees.

Plate any one of the large, moveable sections into which the Earth's surface is divided. Over millions of years, collisions between the plates form new mountains or troughs in the ocean.

Plateau a large, relatively flat area that rises above the surrounding land.

Puna a treeless plateau in the Andes covered in scrubby grass.

Rain forest area of dense, broad-leafed evergreen trees and vines that receives at least 80 inches (200 cm) of rainfall per year.

Selva a wet, dense forest found both in valleys, and on the lower slopes of mountains that surround them.

Shantytown a poor town, or section of a town, where people live in crudely built structures.

Species a type of organism; animals or plants in the same species look similar and can only breed successfully among themselves.

Terrace a step dug into a hillside to create a strip of flat land for planting crops.

Tropical belonging to a geographic region between two imaginary lines drawn around the Earth—the Tropic of Cancer, at 23.5 degrees north of the Equator, and the Tropic of Capricorn, at 23.5 degrees south of the Equator.

Viceroyalty a historical area ruled by a viceroy on behalf of a monarch.

Vulnerable describes a species that is at risk of becoming endangered.

Bibliography

Crowder, Nicholas. *Culture Shock! Peru*. London: Kuperard, 2003.

Gruber, Beth. *Ancient Inca*. Washington, D.C.: National Geographic Society, 2006.

http://www.national geographic.com/mummy/ (Ice Treasures of the Inca)

http://www.peru.info/ e_ftogeneraleng.asp (Official government site for the promotion of Peru)

http://www.lonelyplanet.com/ worldguide/destinations/ south-america/peru// (Lonely Planet travel information)

http://countrystudies.us/peru/ (Library of Congress Country Studies series)

Further Information

NATIONAL GEOGRAPHIC Articles

Banks, Joan. "Journey into the Wild." NATIONAL GEOGRAPHIC WORLD (March 1999): 9–12.

Cayo, Jorge Riveros. "A Taste of Lima." NATIONAL GEOGRAPHIC TRAVELER (July/August 2006): 33.

Eeckhout, Peter. "Ancient Peru's Power Elite." NATIONAL GEOGRAPHIC (March 2005): 52–57.

Howells, Robert Earle. "Discoveries Above the Clouds." NATIONAL GEOGRAPHIC ADVENTURE (May/June 2000): 32–36.

Lange, Karen E. "A Vote for Democracy." NATIONAL GEOGRAPHIC (November 2004): Geographica.

Lanting, Frans, and Maggie Zackowitz. "Be the Animal." NATIONAL GEOGRAPHIC KIDS (September 2003): 32.

Miller, Carrie. "Real Culture." NATIONAL GEOGRAPHIC TRAVELER (September 2002): 66.

Musgrave, Ruth. "Go On Safari! Destination: South America." NATIONAL GEOGRAPHIC KIDS (September 2006): 34–35.

Reinhard, Johan. "Peru's Ice Maidens: Unwrapping the Secrets." NATIONAL GEOGRAPHIC (June 1996): 62–81.

Williams, A.R. "Mystery of the Tattooed Mummy." NATIONAL GEOGRAPHIC (June 2006): 70–83.

Web sites to explore

More fast facts about Peru, from the CIA (Central Intelligence Agency):

https://www.cia.gov/cia/ publications/factbook/geos/ pe.html

Curious about Peru's cities? Go to the Peruvian Embassy's guide for travelers: http:// www.peruvianembassy. us/visiting-peru-destination- guide.php

Intrigued by the Inca Ice Mummies? Learn all about them: www.pbs.org/wgbh/nova/ icemummies

Want to know how El Niño impacts not just Peru but the whole Pacific? http://www. nationalgeographic.com/ elnino/mainpage.html

For more about Peru's native peoples, try this: http://www. peoplesoftheworld.org/text? people=Quichua

Index

Credits

Picture Credits

Front Cover—Top: Sunday morning market in Chincheros, in Peru's highlands; Low Far Left: La Compania church in Plaza de Armas, Lima; Low Left: Inca ruins at Machu Picchu; Low Right: Pottery portrait jug made by the Warí culture; Low Far Right: A llama in the Andean highlands

Page 1—A Quechua-speaking Indian and her baby in Cusco; Icon image on spine, contents page, and throughout: Traditional Andean textiles

Produced through the worldwide resources of the National Geographic Society

John M. Fahey, Jr., *President and Chief Executive Officer*; Gilbert M. Grosvenor, *Chairman of the Board*; Nina D. Hoffman, *Executive Vice President, President of Book Publishing Group*

National Geographic Staff for this Book

Nancy Laties Feresten, *Vice President, Editor-in-Chief of Children's Books*
Bea Jackson, *Director of Design and Illustration*
Virginia Koeth, *Project Editor*
Lori Epstein, *Illustrations Editor*
Stacy Gold, Nadia Hughes, *Illustrations Research Editors*
Carl Mehler, *Director of Maps*
Priyanka Lamichhane, *Assistant Editor*
R. Gary Colbert, *Production Director*
Lewis R. Bassford, *Production Manager*
Vincent P. Ryan, Maryclare Tracy, *Manufacturing Managers*

Brown Reference Group plc. Staff for this Book

Project Editor: Sally MacEachern
Designer: Dave Allen
Picture Manager: Becky Cox
Maps: Martin Darlinson
Artwork: Darren Awuah
Index: Kay Ollerenshaw
Senior Managing Editor: Tim Cooke
Design Manager: Sarah Williams
Children's Publisher: Anne O'Daly
Editorial Director: Lindsey Lowe

About the Author

DR. ANITA CROY earned her Ph.D in Spanish and Latin American studies at University College, United Kingdom. She has traveled extensively in Latin America and has written a number of books for children and young adults on various Latin American countries.

About the Consultants

DR. HILDEGARDO CÓRDOVA AGUILAR is professor of geography and director of the Center for Research in Applied Geography at the Pontifica Universidad Católica del Perú. Born and raised in a mountain community in Piura, he studied at the University of San Marcos in Lima, where he also taught for thirty years. He received his Ph.D in geography from the University of Wisconsin-Madison. He is on the editorial board of the *Journal of Latin American Geography*.

DR. DAVID J. ROBINSON is Dellplain Professor of Latin American Geography at the Maxwell School, Syracuse University. He earned a Ph.D. in Geography from University College London. He is currently editor of the *Journal of Latin American Geography*, and coeditor of the *Journal of Historical Geography*. He has won a number of awards, including a Fulbright-Hays scholarship to do research in Peru and the Eminent Latin Americanist Career Award from the Association of American Geographers.

Time Line of
Peruvian History

B.C.

7500 First village settlements built in Peru.

ca 1200 First identifiable culture emerges in Peru, the Chavín. They later build one of Peru's earliest temple complexes, at Chavín de Huantar, and create a large empire.

ca 100 The Moche come to power over a large area of Peru. The empire is notable for the portrait jars made by its potters, who display individuals with lively features.

A.D.

ca 50 A powerful Moche ruler is buried at Sipán with his attendant and a sacrificial llama. The tomb later becomes one of the most famous Peruvian archaeological sites.

ca 50 In southern Peru, the Nasca begin drawing the mysterious designs in the desert known as the Nasca Lines.

ca 500 The Tiwanaku and Wari rule powerful empires from the highland region near Lake Titicaca.

ca 1000 The Chimú rule much of coastal Peru from a vast adobe city at Chan Chan. They will be one of the most powerful rivals of the Inca.

1400

1438 Inca territorial expansion begins. The Inca leader Yupanqui changes his name to Pachacuti and makes Cusco the ceremonial, political, and economic center of an Inca state.

1460 Pachacuti builds Machu Picchu, a ceremonial center in the Urubamba River valley.

1463 Topa Inca, Pachacuti's son, expands the Inca empire to extend from Quito to central Chile.

1500

1527 War begins between Huayna Capac's sons Huascar and Atahualpa over who should occupy the Inca throne.

1532 Atahualpa's forces kill Huascar, and Francisco Pizarro lands in Peru.

1533 After imprisoning him for a year, the Spanish kill Atahualpa and set up an Inca puppet government.

1534 The Spanish invade Cusco.

1541 A civil war between Spanish settlers leads to the killing of Francisco Pizarro.

1542 Spain declares Colombia, Ecuador, Bolivia, and north-central Argentina to be the Viceroyalty of Peru, and Lima is its capital.

1572 Toledo orders the execution of Tupa Amaru, the last Inca royal heir. The Spanish force the Inca nobility to leave Cusco.

1700

1780 Tupa Amaru II, who claims to be descended from last Inca ruler, leads a rebellion against the Spanish that fails.